Larry D. Thomas
New and Selected Poems

DeDICaTIon
For my DauGHTer, Deena
anD
For my WIFe, LIsa

Larry D. Thomas
New and Selected Poems

TCU Press
Fort Worth, Texas

TCU Texas Poets Laureate Series

Library of Congress Cataloging-in-Publication Data

Thomas, Larry D., 1947-
 [Poems. Selections]
 New and selected poems / Larry D. Thomas.
     p. cm. -- (TCU Texas poets laureate series)
  ISBN 978-0-87565-360-0 (alk. paper)
 1. Title.

PS3620.H63A6 2008
811'.6--dc22

                                   2007042700

This book is made possible by a generous Vision in Action grant from TCU.
Book design by Tom Martens at fusion29. www.fusion29.com

table of contents

INTRODUCTION

Larry D. Thomas of Houston is a fine choice for Texas Poet Laureate, in part, because of the excellence of his body of work. A mature poet, he has an extraordinary gift, which has evolved through decades at his craft.

He also makes an appropriate poet laureate because his pieces are often set in our state. From the natural world, readers find Herefords, cicadas, hawks, and a den or two of rattlesnakes. Indeed, rattlers rank high in Larry Thomas's poetic pantheon.

And geography is certainly there: the Davis Mountains, Palo Duro Canyon, the Trans-Pecos, the Neches River, and the Gulf Coast, to name five places of legend. Furthermore, one encounters familiar sensibilities in pieces where no specific reference exists. Even these sure seem Texas.

I should add that this collection also includes such non-Lone Star concepts as Michelangelo, Beethoven, Georgia O'Keeffe (okay, so O'Keeffe briefly lived in the Panhandle), and Picasso.

Although Larry Thomas must know his way around our heartland and borders, he articulates something for readers everywhere. He goes far beyond a local colorist or chamber of commerce propagandist.

His work hardly parallels the mindset of these wonderfully wrong-headed lines found in the old poem / song, "Beautiful Texas," by lyricist and politician, W. Lee O'Daniel:

> You have all read the beautiful story
> Of countries far over the sea,
> From whence came our ancestors
> To establish this home of the free.
> There are some people who still like to travel

To see what they have over there

But when they go look, it's not like the book

And they find there is none to compare.

To beautiful, beautiful Texas . . .

People still wanting to travel—damn, will they ever learn? Thomas's personal geography is more akin to the universal Louisiana of Kate Chopin than the xenophobic Texas of Pappy O'Daniel. Like Kate Chopin, Larry Thomas captures the spirit of a place within some larger truth that travels well.

Take these first lines from Larry Thomas's poem, "The Red Raging Waters":

For weeks on end it has rained in Texas

sending the Brazos miles beyond its banks

where it rises even now under dark Texas skies

over the wooden floor of a bottomland Baptist church,

floating creaking pews shaped with the aching buttocks

of generations, the wild Brazos rising higher yet

to the stained-glass robes of the Apostles . . .

Deft alliteration and assonance, just right compression of language, diction like few poets can come up with, and yes, each stanza takes you there.

All so authentic. You, the reader, do enjoy this book for its very real Texas elements, yet save some psychic energy for the worldly art here within.

I.
Laden with Red Earth

WIND

(Circa 1880, West Texas)

It died down to a zephyr
but would never, never stop.
All they did was listen
and grace it now and then
with psalms and gospels.
Its dogged struggle

was a perfect metaphor
for their faith, the manner,
even for their memory,
in which it kept after them,
sanding their gravestones
night and day to dust.

When the sky greened and it rose,
in case it made a cyclone,
they grabbed their kids and hurried
down the steps of their cellars,
armed with but hard prayer
to foil the howling darkness.

PALO DURO CANYON

A straight
razor,
this wind
of winter

scraping
high plains
till they bleed,
scraping

toward a canyon
where cedar clings
to sheer faces
of cliffs,

clawing roots
into hard
red scabs
of earth,

this wind
of winter
scraping its way
to a canyon rim

where hawks,
slingshot-flung,
scream in dazzling
Texas sun.

Herefords in Winter

It's nine degrees above zero.
They stand still in the pasture, staring
at nothing but the barbs of taut wire,

the sky above them so blue and cold
even the hawks have taken shelter.
They stare chewing their cud

against a distant backdrop of cap rock
their white faces hover over
like full, haunting moons familiar with sky

and the feeble daily scaldings
of the sun. They stare straight through
their barbed and lone existences,

surviving the cold,
flourishing in their heaven
of bleakness.

THE RED RAGING WATERS

For weeks on end it has rained in Texas
sending the Brazos miles beyond its banks
where it rises even now under dark Texas skies

over the wooden floor of a bottomland Baptist church,
floating creaking pews shaped with the aching buttocks
of generations, the wild Brazos rising higher yet

to the stained-glass robes of the Apostles,
soaking the feet of Jesus and lapping the elbows
of His uplifted arms, creeping up the pulpit

on whose open Bible coils a fat diamondback,
the red raging waters of the Brazos
bringing to sweet communion the serpent and the saint.

Rattlesnake Roundup

At sunrise, bands of gunless hunters
stud the bleak, West Texas landscape,
clutching forked sticks, wide-eyed at openings
of cap rock dens, shoving vees

behind the venom-bulged heads of vipers,
bagging their catch in coarse tow sacks
for the trip to the town coliseum,
to pits teeming with fugues of fierce rattling

where handlers press fangs against lips of jars,
milking poison, and butchers section cuts
for deep fryers, cooking sweet, snow-white meat
for the leathery mouths of old townsfolk.

"OF DUST THOU ART"

In Van Horn, in far West Texas,
the sun has turned their faces
into deep red leathery brains.
They breathe dry air laden with red earth,

their lungs the lower halves
of rubbery hourglasses
turning year by sedulous year,
right before their eyes, into dust.

Even the hard oaken pews
they sit on during worship are dust-filmed
where they wheeze with clotted breath
the strains of "Amazing Grace."

Evenings, after the sun
has wobbled like a glob
down the rock-and-cactus-fleshed slopes
of mountains their forebears named Diablo,

they take to their gritty beds,
ease the quilts of grandmas
over their leathery bodies
like slabs of red earth, and they pray.

Rain

What few times it did come
it came down all at once,
the entire sky conspiring
to dump its blue in buckets

squarely on them, drowning
their cattle in arroyos, knocking
their fence posts to the ground,
so alien to the parched Trans-Pecos

that when it struck at midnight
pounding their roofs
of corrugated metal like thousands
of tiny ball-peen hammers,

they bolted from their beds,
fell to their knees, and prayed
their God would spare them
from the vile, freezing spit of Satan.

THE SKULL SELLER

(Terlingua, far West Texas)

She said she'd lived
there all her life.
As she spoke, a wisp
of white dust engulfed us,

brushed from the skulls
of steers she scoured
for bleaching by the sun.
Her eyes were the palest

blue I'd ever seen,
bleached as the skulls
tagged and shelved for sale.
She rambled on about

the vast Chihuahuan
Desert, how it baked them
in the low-heat oven
of the sun, leathering

flesh over time
for rasping by the ever
present wind, for the rasping
of their skulls to mortars,

their bones to pestles
pounding them down
to the powder
of blinding light.

vultures

To make them
God took
the thick
black fabric
of shadows
and tore it
into shreds.

With the cloths
of their beaks,
they buff
the bones
of the dead
to a fine
white shine,

and they roost,
sagging
the branches
of dead trees
with the droopy,
sated yearnings
of their bodies.

Texas Mountain Laurel

In early spring,
for a distance
of several feet,

it wafts the aroma
of the thick, sweet
juice of grapes.

Its branches creak
and sway, laden
with the cascading

clusters of blooms
teeming with bees
like monks in amber

robes, intoxicated
with contemplation,
humming their chants,

rapt in fragrant
monasteries
of lavender.

over Barbecue

Too old to work cattle, they gather
once in a while around a campfire

fueled with dead mesquite to swap tales
over barbecue. One asks the eldest

how many steers he supposes
he's eaten in his life. He muses

a few seconds and answers surely
a sizable herd. Their dentures

clack tearing meat from spareribs, loose
as the clothes on their gaunt, bent frames.

Each chomps on, adding another head
to the ghostly, sizable herd

roaming the horizons of his marrow,
lowing in the pasture of his soul.

Amazing Grace

As both generations of the blood kin before her,
Grace has lived her life on her grandfather's spread.
She's never cared as much for the townsfolk
as the barren majesty of the land itself.
She's never even thought about leaving.
It's as if she herself were fashioned from its clay,
eased by a shovel from her mother's womb

and blessed some way with the miracle of breath.
In her withered spinsterhood, long retired
from her forty years of teaching high school English,
she still rises before first light
and takes her place in her porch rocker.
When moonless, her night sky's a black
velvet jeweler's cloth of roiling solitaires.

Among the adults of her West Texas hamlet,
she's lived her life a closet sophisticate,
just to keep down trouble. Perhaps that's why
she rises every day before dawn for the breaking
of light so intense it's palpable; warm, amber light
savory as the brandy of aged literature
swirling in the snifter of her skull.

ALZHEIMER'S

She first heard its onset
in the sudden, *staccato*
rhythm of her speech,
in the gradual diminishing
of brilliant memory

from chord to *arpeggio.*
Though largely confined
to the minimalist composition
of her nursing home room,
she still insists that the aide

help her daily with a black gown
and wrap her hair in a bun.
Positioned on her bench
with the straight-backed posture
she assumed as a concert pianist,

she sits at her only window
and watches the *diminuendo* of light
from afternoon to evening,
evening to dusk, and dusk
to the endlessly repeated

étude of the night,
each of her long,
slender fingers
swaying like the winding down
needle of a metronome.

TEXAS TWO-STEP

For sixty some odd years,
he worked cattle. His backbone's
bowed like a divining rod
urgent for water,
pulling his face toward the dust.

Having outlived all his children,
he still somehow manages
to live alone. In far West Texas,
in the land of his ancestors,
he lives in his centenarian

world where dreams and consciousness
are partners in a polka.
Nights, prior to retiring,
after the wind has died
and dust has settled

on his corrugated iron roof
like the laying on of hands,
he shoves his boots
under the cane-bottomed chair
beside his bed.

Mornings, regaining consciousness
like a slowly developing
negative, he neither knows nor cares,
till his boots come into focus,
whether he's still in the dance.

MADONNA AND CHILD

The cathedral rises from the earth
like the sheer rock face of a mountain.
From its lofty perch in the belfry,
the raven gazes at the beggar

on the street below. She is kneeling,
covered completely by her black cloak,
reaching through a fold her cupped,
clawed hand, lifeless as a wooden ladle.

With what dignity she begs,
uttering not a word, nodding her thanks
in utter darkness for a single *peso.*
She'll stay this way for hours in the sun,

making under her cloak the sign of the cross
to each passerby, praying in silence
for that most blessed of His miracles
turning meal into milk

for the toothless gums of her infant.
As she prays the raven shudders,
ruffling its feathers, ringing the bells
of their elegant darkness.

THE LIGHT OF MEXICO

It's no wonder the painters
love it so: the way,
in little villages,
it brings out the pinks, greens,

blues, yellows, and lavenders
of humble houses
dazzling the flanks of mountains
like strewn fruit: the way,

at zero hour, suits of it
mesmerize the eyes of bulls:
the way, as if from nowhere,
it sparkles the dark,

chocolate eyes of mothers
so comfortable with death
they candy its skulls
for the tongues of bronze children.

EL camino del rio

Low-water crossings,
loose livestock, steep grades
and sharp curves are common
along this scenic drive
beside the Rio Grande
between Lajitas and Presidio.

The river, patient
as a sedulous sculptor
spellbound for thousands of years
by his work, employing
his single utensil of water,
has carved walls of stone

towering hundreds of feet.
The Apaches knew them
as the places of no return. Only
the screams of hawks, bouncing
ad infinitum off the canyon walls,
sound as if they belong.

KALEIDOSCOPE

morning in Santa Fe
of breathtaking brightness
when even the petals

of the flowers children pluck
are stained glass ablaze with sunlight;
when the sky pulsates in the bathed,

inscrutable eyes of young women;
when adulterers luxuriate
under the chocolate gaze of a priest

and the bronze, wrinkled skin
of Indians blooms silver
studded with chunks of polished turquoise;

when, rising in their homes of adobe,
the old women open their shutters
and gasp in flashfloods of light.

warrior woman

At night,
among the ancient kachinas
in the tomb-like silence
of the museum,
looms this dark little doll

of pure spirit
carved of cottonwood root
with a flake of stone,
painted with a brush
of stiff yucca fiber.

Her face is black,
her mouth a rectangle
lined in red,
filled with six triangles
of sharp white teeth.

For hundreds of years
she has stood rock-still,
staring down the darkness
with the bright yellow circles
of her eyes.

For Purity

(for Georgia O'Keeffe)

she dons jet-black
and takes her stance
before the canvas,

draping her heart
with the shadow
of a black cross.

She scours her mind
with cloudless
desert sky,

and she waits
for the moon-like rising
of the flower,

the pelvis,
the cleansed,
sun-bleached skull.

Bones

O'Keeffe found them
rendered so immaculate
by the sun and wind
it was as if someone,
with bleach and the bristles
of a steel brush,

had scoured them clean.
In the winter of her life,
as she strolled the desertscapes
of Ghost Ranch with her cane
and beloved black chow chow,
she must have felt her own

reaching for the light, pressing
against her skin from within,
seeking in the clear
New Mexican air
the music of radiant
bleaching by the sun.

II.
The Gray Fabric of the Sky

Neches River

It moves along the bottom
of deep East Texas
like the minute hand over the face
of an antique grandfather clock,

turgid with its prehistoric
cargo of gators and seven-foot gars
waving their fins in utter darkness.
A wild sow

tests it with her cloven hoof,
takes the plunge, and heads across it
with her three terrified shoats.
Soon, in absolute silence,

it will swallow them whole,
smooth out the frantic ripples
of their passage, and flow on,
keeping as it has for hundreds of years

its turbid, lugubrious time.

SLUG

Having shed
the shell of the snail
through the grueling
parsimony of evolution,

it's the darkness
itself, animate.
The night is its castle
and it the queen

so accomplished
in its arrogance
it dares not even walk
but chooses instead

to shuffle its every move
along the plush,
clear carpet
of its mucus.

IN THE VOODOO LOUNGE

An hour after showtime,
the lights go out.

An old black man
navigates the glow
of black lights,
and eases his buttocks
to the woven
cane bottom of a chair.

His knobby,
sharecropper fingers
clutch a pick
and curl
around the long,
fretted neck
of his Fender.

A riff
surges through the darkness
like neon gas
through a glass tube.

One by one,
fierce black lions
leap from the steel
of plucked strings,
ripping sodden hearts
with the unsheathed
claws of the blues.

TWIN SPINSTERS IN BLUE

It's an early
December morning
an hour after sunrise.
The quiet streets
alongside Cherryhurst Park
are completely canopied
with the branches of oaks
hundreds of years old.
Their long blue-black coats
sashed at their waists,
they sit at the center
of the park in the sun,
their navy blue canes
angled against their bench.
They can count
on their gloved fingers
the words which pass between them,
having long survived
the last of their living kin.
They spend their days this way,
acting out the script
of simple ritual,
the deep sky above them
familiar at last
as the blue silk handkerchiefs
creased inside their purses.

Tumescence

The clouds, protuberant
with the urgency of rain,
sag the gray fabric

of the sky. Her nostrils,
swollen with fluid, flare
with the scent of biscuits

rising in the wood stove.
The slats of her rocker
bow under the heaviness

of imminent birthing.
Her hand, weary from tracing
the aching curvature

of her twelve-pound, past-due son,
dangles near a rosebush
whose burgeoning pinks, poised

as the scalpels of surgeons,
start splitting the drum-
stretched sheaths of their buds,

the possibility
of a Caesarean section
remote as lights, running water.

THE LAWS OF HIS KIND

are mutable as the changing faces
of the alpha males.
His gravestone but the camouflage
of a thick blanket

of loblolly needles,
he lies like a mummy
in a wrap of doeskin
bound by the calloused hands

which stilled his breathing.
He lies under several feet
of the rich, black humus
they're all destined to,

staring down the darkness
with his three, wide-open eyes,
his mercifully orchestrated death
eternally uncertified as his birth.

CROWS ROOSTING

The winter sky is numinous,
overcast with layers of cloud-gauze
wrapped loosely around the luminous
oozing wound of Sunday morning.

The leaves, what few remain
of the Chinese tallow,
have capitulated to a stain
of oxblood, burgundy, and harvest gold,

hanging by their stems for dear life
and an imminent pirouette to death.
Deep within the leaves' tenuous strife
they roost, these priests and priestesses

of darkness, blue-black with blight,
preening the sheen of their plumes,
each a grim reminder of the night
making the morning so terribly bright.

# of ceremony

The garments
are shreds of dark,
dilated pupils.

The colors closing in,
he quakes in the bowels
of ceremony,

and smells the burnt altar
of the dog,
his own body

a violent engine
whose boiling blood-oil
keeps burning itself out.

He takes the meat and eats
to the scarlet drums
of a human heart.

In sleep
he blends wild flesh
with his blood,

taking unto himself
the howl, the pack,
the sure, skilled kill.

EVEN THE MOON

He's just become
a brother.
Even the moon

is full,
and he feels
his proud colors

gleaming on the back
of a sleeveless,
denim jacket.

Even the moon
is full
and his dark soul

satiate
with the sanctity
of taboo.

Under his colors,
in his flesh,
the vacuous eyes

of a raw, winged skull
brim with tears
of fresh blood.

A BIG BLACK RAVEN

Astraddle their wide-
open Harleys,
they ravish
the moonlit night,

each frayed thread
of denim,
each gleaming
human hair cracking

like a little whip
as they ride as one
in the tried honor
of a brother,

each skull aching
from a ruffling
of feathers
in a nasty nest

where mind's naught
but shredded carrion
for a big black raven
of revenge.

colors

sear flesh
with mild fever
as brothers sleep

in the warmth
of a grave
brotherhood,

and dream
of dark hearts
beating

with one pulse,
each pierced ear
poised

for the knocking
of an old self's
knuckles

bloodying
at a door
of skulls.

THaT GLOrIOUS CrasH

Without a helmet
he rides the night
ever fast,
his hair the feathers

of hawks diving,
even faster
till he and the wind
are nothing but murmurs

of the same truth,
faster still
till his bike gives way
to the quiet pavement

and he's airborne
like a fat, wingless crow
hurtling to earth
for that glorious crash

when human bones break
to give marrow
a gift of night air
and torn flesh

floods wild fields
with thick rivers
of human blood,
all for the crash,

the passing out,
the dark coming to
between stark, white sheets
of survival.

THE SOFT LAMPS

of bodies
whose nostril hairs
are the strings of harps
darkened by the strumming

of meaty breath,
of bodies
entranced in shadow-song
where slabs of cave rock

rife with blue drawings
are dreamed into flesh
whose human fur
fumes of celebration,

of bodies
moonstruck, deep sleep-fallen,
anointed
with meaty oil.

SHe WOrKS NIGHTS

when bikers ride
and sleeps days
under black silk sheets.

Some creature of darkness
milked a crescent moon
for her skin

which cringes from a sun
scraping her window shades
with sharp yellow claws.

Under the bright lizard lids
of her eyes,
she dreams of herself dancing

in a thousand dark lounges,
her only havens
of constant night,

their cool, blue bulbs of light
all she'll ever nurse
of sun or pallid virtue.

CRABBER

Ninety years of Galveston sun
reign in her flesh like a bronze tattoo
needled indelibly into her face,
arms, and legs. Her throat's adorned
with a choker of perfect shark teeth,
hard, imperturbable as her squinty gaze.
Daily, during the summer months,

she takes fresh chicken necks, yanks string
around them tight as tourniquets,
grabs net and bucket and prances
the few yards from her shanty to the surf.
With nothing but her sense of touch, she works
her stringed necks like a master, easing
the net under the bellies of greedy crabs

and shaking them violently
to the bottom of her bucket. As she waits
for the next strike, she fixes her gaze
on the sea, matching its brute indifference
with the iciness of her stare,
the crabs clacking in the bucket like dominoes
shuffled by the age-blotched hands of old men,

fueling her dream of dropping big blue males
into a bubbling stockpot flaring her nostrils
with crab-boil, reddening their blue
in but minutes, their sweet, white meat
but briefly satisfying to her appetite
as the seven feckless husbands
whose cremated bodies she's dumped into the sea.

Brown Pelican

Of sticks of driftwood from God knows where,
rotting patches of shrimpers' nets,

bits of the sea-stained Styrofoam of old floats,
strands of mooring rope wrapping the down

of dead gulls and halves of dead crabs' pincers,
and crumbling remnants of the corks

of voyaged bottles, she crafted her nest
where she ruffles her feathers and sits,

oblivious to mites marching through her plumes
like battalions of a tiny Russian army,

the pliant webbing of her pouch
tucked under her bill like the countless chins

of a corpulent diva basking in the sun,
reveling in the fish-fragrant glory of her self.

GHOST CraB

The meat beneath its pale
yellowish carapace
but the substance
of spirit,
it lies perfectly still
inches below the mouth
of its hole.

But the devil's reach away,
at high tide,
black waves quake the beach
like the dropped barbells
of weight lifters.
To the drumbeat
of each wave,

the tiny psalm
of its body shudders
with nothing
to ward off the darkness
but the raised
white pincers
of its prayer.

OLD GULL

It drags its broken wing like a bad divorce.
God only knows how it's lasted
so many weeks this way, the soar

far from its reach as requited love.
It survives by staying close
to the sea, the faithful webbing

of its feet all it can count on
to flee the grasp of feral cats.
The cruel winter wind

plasters its feathers to its breast,
twisting nearly off its dangling wing
scribbling on the beach

the undecipherable hieroglyphs
of its fate, its glaucous eyes
unblinking, fixed on the rising tide

reaching toward it like a savior
to wash sparklingly clean
its agonizing slate of survival.

in the nacreous hours

(September 1900, Galveston, Texas)

before the Great Storm of 1900,
a calm breeze rustles palm fronds
like cotton castanets. The evening sky
is opalescent, disturbed by nothing

but the glides, swoops, and dives of gulls.
The children are nonchalant,
licking their bright red lollipops,
stuffing their mouths with sticky

pink wads of cotton candy.
The waves, grown mysteriously angry,
strike shell beds with the opening notes
of Beethoven's *Fifth*. The puppet limbs

of lovers are thrashing in the sky,
the cotton threads of their lifelines
twisting, fraying, held by but the screaming
of the brute, careening gulls.

The Ferry

It's amazing how it even floats,
constructed as it is of steel,
concrete and macadam
and loaded to capacity

with dump trucks, eighteen wheelers
and faded station wagons
creaking with the lineage
of three or more generations.

Gulls eager for a handout
swoop, dive and void at its stern
while the riders at its bow
keep turning their other

chapped, wind-puffed cheeks
to the lashes of cold salt spray.
Day in and day out it churns,
moving its riders from island

to peninsula, peninsula to island,
brooking their absurdities
for twenty or so minutes,
and then, like the lumbering,

nauseous whale of Jonah,
vomiting them up
to the stark, uncharted
beaches of their lives.

FROM THE DARK SWELLS

It's the night
of the day
of the sentencing
of their brother.

They kill their Harleys
at the sea's edge.
The black sea
and their heavy, black hearts
beat to the same,
bleak music.

This moonless night
the sea is calm,
itself a huge, black robe
of cruel justice.

Seaward,
from the dark swells,
two gulls emerge
like the trembling, white hands
of the judge,

reaching for the verdict.

THE LIGHTHOUSE KEEPER

It rises from the peninsula
like a black, rounded obelisk,
jutting through the fog, lifting but a memory
of its once bright light to sparkle

the distant, salt-stung eyes of tired seamen.
The local children swear on crossed hearts
that his ghost still haunts its dark interior,
tending the light, guiding gaunt mariners

he knows he'll never meet to the momentary
safety of the harbor. On moonless nights,
in their dreams, the children faintly see
the swaying lantern of his final trek

down the steep spiral staircase of his life
as he lumbers toward the ink black sea,
the children jerking in their sleep
to the thudding of his peg leg on each steel step,

knocking on the door of heaven.

III.

Legions of Blue Angels

OUT OF THE BLUE

But for the three of us,
the park that day was deserted.
Mom meant no harm
and said she was just kidding
when, out of the blue,
she sped off in the Buick
and left me and my little brother
stranded on the blanket
we'd spread for a picnic.
Beyond the elm-shaded acres
of Cole Park, in far West Texas,
the flat red earth
ran unobstructed for miles
in all four directions,
all the way to the horizon.
Sam clutched his teddy bear
and started crying.
I stood in my white,
suspendered shorts
and watched the car
dissolve in a cloud of dust.
A few minutes later,
when she drove back,
I was still standing,
too shocked to speak or cry,
dispossessed at three of my trust,
held against her heaving chest
weightless as the husk
of a cicada.

Gabriel

He lived with his grandparents
on the corner of our block.
The neighborhood kids
taunted him with clods.

Their parents, over coffee
before their children woke,
said if he'd been theirs
they'd have aborted him.

Late one summer evening,
he cautiously approached me,
mumbling words only
his grandparents understood,

nodded for me to follow.
He led me to his backyard,
stooped to pick up his prized,
miniature horse,

and asked in words
painstakingly voiced
as if that very moment
he were hewing them from stone,

if I would like
to hold his horse
for just a little while,
before it got too dark.

A Place in the Sun

When a dutiful child,
I sat on my pew with folded hands
like a strange piñata
layered with the onion-
skin pages of my Bible.

As I grew up, the layers
dried and cracked wide-open,
oozing the pungent
smelling salts of recognition,
drawing me up, against my will,

in the middle of communion,
from the hard oaken pew
of my chrysalis
and leading me up the aisle
and outside to take my rightful place

in the sun, shocking the congregation
with my ostensible irreverence
though I stood in the bright hot light
more consonant with Jesus
than I'd ever been.

OF FATHERS AND SONS

One summer morning, an hour before first light,
when Mom and Dad thought I was asleep,
I woke to the bubbling and the scent

of percolating Folgers and a portion
of soft conversation seeping ghostlike
through the thin wooden panel of my door.

The day before, Dad and I had argued
violently about his never telling me
he loved me. He said it was ludicrous,

that I should find more than adequate
his seven-day workweek at his filling station.
I blurted I didn't. He retorted, "Tough."

We then went back to work, he under
the grease rack, I in the carwash stall. I felt
hurt, started washing the cars harder.

In my bed, I heard him tell Mom how proud
of me he was, how he'd never seen a man
wash as many cars in a twelve-hour

day. It gave me chills, so much I just lay there
frozen till sunrise. Years later, moments before
their joint burial, I let them know I heard.

OF EYES WONDROUSLY WILD

(for Lisa)

Clawing the street
under the tree of its birth,
it lay there on asphalt
cooling with shadows of evening.
Limp at its side

hung its broken wing
auguring hidden injuries
ridiculously accidental
and far too soon, fatal.
I eased it with great care

to the cupped left hand
of my wife. With her right
index finger she stroked it
in a futile human attempt
to soothe the dark terrors

of eyes wondrously wild
for the fleeting little seconds
of a life. It blinked
once or twice, shuddered, and died,
her cupped hand its warm coffin.

My wife's eyes watered
and a breeze came,
lifting her hair from her cheeks
like the soft, glorious wings
of ascension.

Harvest Moon

(for Deena)

It hung in the late
October sky
so big and bright
people everywhere,
just to look at it,
pulled their cars
over to the shoulders
of the roads.

My daughter of two,
clung to my chest
like a monkey,
caught suddenly up
in the throes
of her small body
acting with a mind
of its own, pointed her right

index finger toward the sky,
parted her pursed lips,
and crooned, for the very
first time, sliding off her tongue
like a warm, sweet disk
of butterscotch candy,
the word "moon," startling
her so she started crying.

primary colors

(for Deena, in memory of my mother)

For several months,
Mom's clinical depression
had kept her indoors.
She killed time
drifting through her universe

of drugs, clad
in but her gown
and pale blue housecoat
she kept buttoning
below her knees, for prudence.

One late October day,
after a blue norther
had passed through town,
rubbing the sky
to raw cobalt,

my daughter of three
led her by her pinkie
to the backyard,
got her to lie down
in the grass,

and buried
all but the cameo
of her face
under a foot or more
of red and yellow leaves,

believing,
with all her heart,
that that many reds and yellows
couldn't help but thaw
her grandma's blues.

THE NIGHT WE WERE GODS

They hung by thread
just above our heads
in the entryway,
five hummingbirds
of clear red glass

covered with glitter.
Absentmindedly,
we brushed them
with the tips
of our forefingers,

rubbed our eyelids
and smeared them
with galaxies
of tiny stars.
For several hours,

till we showered,
and never even
noticing, we blessed
everything we touched
with crushed light.

Artificial Fruit

I saw them in a basket
on the table, in a slant

of late afternoon, winter
sunlight, a scrumptious cluster

of apricots so fresh their stems
were still attached, bearing, trembling

in a current of air from a vent,
browning leaves curling in the act

of dying. I stood there bothered
by their symmetry, too perfect

for actual fruit, so I bent
toward them, checking for redolence

or a bruise. Their plastic smell
gave them away, the telltale

sign of fraud. I felt a sadness
in their unbridgeable distance

from the real, imagining
their hollow desire, their longing

to trade their everlasting beauty
for even the transitory

dirge of decay, or clank of the knife
bounded against the stone of life.

BLUING

It came in a little
bottle, so blue it looked
jet-black. I knew it was
nothing but trouble,
the way a tiny

drop of it would turn
a washtub of water
into a huge, sloshing
sapphire. Mama used it,
oddly enough, to whiten

our Sunday shirts.
Over time it bled
right through her skin
and blued her all the way
to commitment

in the Wichita State
Hospital, bleaching
her heart into a locket
white and fragile
as fine bone china.

Aunt Mae and Uncle Worley's Rocker

For the last ten years of his life,
no matter the weather, he shuffled
to his rocker on the porch
to while away his hours.

It sits in the same place
it sat when he died a decade back.
Its presence comforts her:
the way the slats of its seat

slightly sag as if still laden
with his weight; the way at night,
when the wind's just right,
a floorboard creaks with its rocking.

She's left it there to play out
its usefulness, to play with the sun,
in the tournament of dust,
the checkers of light and shadow.

COTTON

It blanketed Mother
in the pale blue
softness of a nightgown;
Dad, the propriety
of a white shirt.

At their request,
even their caskets
were fashioned of it
to aid their swift
reunion with the earth.

For miles around
the cemetery,
red fields of it
lay fallow, fields
where in their youth,

sunup to sundown,
they picked it, each
a hundred pounds a day,
where they picked it
till their fingers bled.

TO BLUE

(in memory of my brother, Sam)

in bleak December,
he loosed his restless soul.
For weeks before he died,
his frail body
propped on a cane,

he scoured countless stores
and antique shops
for blue glass ornaments.
He hung them
on a noble fir

flocked snow-white,
strung with endless
strands of blue lights,
and slept on a cot
beside the tree.

As death descended
in a flock of blue crows,
his blue eyes glistened
with legions of blue angels
blaring their silent horns.

SPIRIT SIGN

(for Lisa)

In the lavender air of dusk,
at the base of a Davis Mountain,
even her loose, cotton blouse
was inked with blooms and sky
the evening she stood with arms
outstretched, each comfortably laden

with the clear, red plastic strawberry
of a feeder brimming with sugary water,
dangling from the grip of forefinger
and thumb, when suddenly out of nowhere
the hummingbirds appeared, buzzing
her body like bees their hallowed hive,

stabbing the clear, red nectar
with the long, curved needles of their beaks,
tattooing her soul with their vivid,
weightless fury, leaving her
breathless, bedazzled, indelible
with the bliss of iridescence.

Driving Through West Texas

Locked for an hour on cruise control
without meeting another vehicle,
I'm hypnotized by yellow
stripes, whizzing by like arrows.

Sixty miles back, I missed the sign
posted by a Mobil Hopper
would've liked, the last gas stop
for the next hundred miles.

The wind howls through my cracked
window. Though moonless, the night
reminds me of the set
of an old Frankenstein flick,

flaring with hundreds of torches.
The Day-Glo reddish-orange
needle of my gas gauge
quivers, almost horizontal.

I swerve to miss a diamondback
slithering across the macadam.
For no clear reason, I say aloud
the word "diamondback."

It startles me, not so much the word
itself but the intimacy
with which I utter it,
as if it were the name of a friend.

ROaD KILL

It's as if they lay there
in the pattern of some dark plan,
spaced as they were on the macadam,
flattened by the sole of a jealous god
for imminent mummification by the sun,
a male and female jackrabbit
catching the corner of my eye at daybreak.

I couldn't help but picture the instant
before their deaths, their eyes all pupil
leading them through the ink black night,
making sudden contact with beams
so bright they had to be celestial,
leaving them hopelessly paralyzed
in the snapshot-quick of rapture.

APRICOTS

A few blocks off the plaza,
in the Santa Fe evening light
the color of brandy,
on the street below the branches

of the tree, they glowed in rosy,
yellow hues as if a god
had ripped the sundown, rolled it
into fuzzy, dimpled balls,

and flung them to the ground.
Fast as we could, deep
into the fabric of our shorts,
we crammed them till our pockets

sagged, and lumbered down
the darkening street
like lumpy angels, holy
with the light of apricots.

IV.

The Simple Things They Cherished (New Poems)

BACH

Encircled
by a baroque design
of oak leaves, acorns
and flowers, his profile's

tooled in brass,
centered in a small
brass plate hanging on the wall.
He faces east, unsmiling,

toward something elusive,
contrapuntal as the melody
of light pouring in daily
through the window,

juxtaposed with shadow
in a silent fugue
building to the climax
of the night.

Hawk

His belly full
of warm,
shredded prey
he knocked
from heaven
with the sledge-

hammer fury
of his dive,
he gazes
from his perch
high above
the wilderness.

It took two
full-time gods
millions of years
to fashion
his beak
and claws.

THE GOLFER

(for Bob Spears)

Daily at daybreak, even in the rain,
I see him in the distance
sinking his tee into the teeing ground,
centering his white ball
snugly in the circle of its cup,
clutching the grip of his driver,
and merging his body and mind
for the drive, a solitary man, who,
with but his clubs, tees, balls and game
of power, grace and touch so precise
he calculates the breath of crows,
plays the farthest reaches of his soul.

Flaking the Slate Gravestones

This Sunday morning in October
a dense fog has settled over Boston
like gray gauze damp with ether,

eased to the breathing of the ill.
I make my way by foot to Cambridge Street,
and I see the street people,

a white man, a black woman,
making love on a concrete mattress
under a tattered gray blanket,

barely moving as I pass yet making love
as if nothing else matters,
neither the nearby Common of Lowell's "...Union Dead"

nor the cascading chimes of Park Street Church
drifting through the mist to Granary Burying Ground,
jarring the bones of Revere, Hancock, Adams,

flaking the slate gravestones
with the rhythmic, invisible chisel
of the hymn.

In Maine

(after Andrew Wyeth)

A dry hill
slopes to the sea.

Night falls.

The kitchen
is abandoned
under the steep pitch
of a roof.

A window
is cracked
for the wind.

A cloud passes
and the light
of a wolf moon
crashes in
like the ax
of God.

French Quarter

(for Deena)

Below sea level, in night fog
thick as chicken and sausage gumbo, it looms,
this whole place a brick and concrete grave
adorned with Spanish and French iron,
a grisly Easter basket

wrapped in alternating bands
of green, gold, and purple cellophane
under which flicker the lights,
the ghastly lights of gas lamps and neon
every hue of the rainbow

illuming the ghostly faces
of voodooienne Marie Laveau
and the Saint Louis Cathedral
sticking its spires into night sky
like pins in a doll of voodoo, voodoo

whose rhythmic chants gave birth to jazz
in this glittering city of sin and Lent
forever gently nudged by the giant python
of the Mississippi, triumphant, tumescent,
and shining from its meal of mice and men.

A Matter of Color

Each of their lives a hue
beautifully strange, inimitable,
the elderly winter here in droves.

Though it's hardly perceptible
from one year to the next,
each of the winters diminishes them,

drawing them just a little
closer to the sand.
Each morning at sunrise,

on the eggshell
of a beach wet with nacre,
they shuffle like crayons

wearing toward a stub, clutched
for a while in the sure,
right hand of God.

woman WITH a crow

(charcoal, pastel and watercolor on paper by Pablo Picasso)

Framed by a flat blue,
she leans on the angle
of her left elbow
resting on a table

where a crow stands.
Her head's hunched
toward the crow, her lips
pressed against its head.

Her long, tapered fingers,
as if caressing,
run the length
of the crow's breast.

Her face is featured
with the stylized
sameness of marble:
her face, hair, hand,

red blouse and neck
all smudged with shadow,
the black, bleeding shadow
of the crow.

THe DraGOnFLY

Through the glass I see a radiant hue.
Inside my writing studio vacant
for several days, a hot shaft of sunlight,
shining through a skylight, illumes the blue
husk of a dragonfly. Last week it flew
into the room. I never noticed it.
All I know is when I left, it didn't,
but died of old age or starvation, too

feeble to last till I returned and dart
for the aperture to sky when I slid
the glass door open. Now, but its blue glows,
emptied of the juice of life, the hard art
of its karma gaudy as the eyelids
of harlots, slathered with sparkling shadow.

CROW WITH RED SKY

(watercolor by Leonard Baskin)

Grossly oversized,
fashioned from the grunts of gods,
its legs are blunt pedestals
for the black marble density

of a body usurping a backdrop
of red sky so violently
its tail's chopped off by the paper's edge.
Its beak's a stubby holocaust

of buffed, black iron.
Black hairs jut from feet and legs
like rebar tips in cured concrete.
It stands on a flat surface

balanced on the points of eight claws
etched with the strength to pierce steel.
All of heaven sparkles
in the closed, black noose of its eye.

coma

For weeks she has languished
like a blank sheet
of stationery, creased,
sealed inside the envelope
of her bedsheets.

Her skin is eggshell,
pale as the petals
of a cut,
long-stemmed rose
suspended in a vase

of tepid water.
Voices, if she hears them
at all, are indistinct,
far away as cymbals
struck beneath the sea.

A faint pulse
flutters in her wrists
like small
blue moths,
hovering.

Minotaur

Though his hands,
by turns,
can chisel *David*
from marble
and execute

the ravishing,
intricate scores
of Beethoven,
he would trade
a thousand

for a single
cloven hoof
to paw the blood-
soaked earth
of a bullring,

his bull's
dark desire
languishing
in the paltry,
flaccid organ

of a man,
ridiculous
for placating
even the gentlest
cow in heat.

TerLinGua

I. Jackrabbit

Silent as gray oil
squeezed from its tube
by a painter,
he oozes from his scrape
onto the blue-black canvas
of the night, the size
of his ears and rear legs
a testament to his terror.

II. Mirage

Looking back at the ranch house
where he was reared, he knows
it seems leftward and above
its true location, shimmering
as it is in waves as if
buckling to the heartless
cobalt pressure of the sky.
To prove it's an illusion,
he snaps it with his camera
but sees it's not. He also sees,
in the image, the shimmering
blue water he knows is fake,
fraudulent as the professor
who posited with seeming
certainty, just last week
in college, a tremulous
definition of reality.

III. It's the City

without limits,
ever unincorporated,
its boundaries so elusive,
so brazen they don't
distinguish Texas
from Mexico.

Its roads are dirt, mainly
unnamed, anonymous
as the scattered denizens
of its ghost town. Even
the origin of its name
is ghostlike, hovering
about the tongues of Mexicans,
Apaches, and Anglos.
Since the mine died, it's lured
eccentrics, loners, and lovers
of creosote, mesquite,
ocotillo, and sundowns
colored with the dust
of crushed crayons.
Its hallowed graveyard,
as much a monument
to Mother Desert as the bones
of the deceased, is haunted
with the troubled souls
of miners, decades dead,
each of whose mouths
is a wavy, Munch oval locked
forever open in the quick-
silver silence of a scream.

IV. The Drifter

In the late night
shadows of El Paso,
he heard muffled gunshots,
looked in their direction,
and saw two men
crumpled in an alley,
one of whom had dropped
a briefcase. Neither man moved,
no one else was around,
so he grabbed the briefcase
and ran. It was filled
with hundred dollar bills,

probably drug money,
he crammed into his duffle bag.
At daybreak, he caught
a ride with a trucker,
was quietly courteous,
and ended up here
where folks, what few
there are, never question
a newcomer.
He's blended like the others
with the desert,
inconspicuous
as the dust whose presence
and whose drifting are one.

V. The Cactus Lady

For years, to keep her true name secret,
she's had her monthly SSI check
direct-deposited in an Alpine bank.
Everyone in Terlingua, even her neighbor,
knows her only as "Cactus Lady."
Around the first of each month
she drives alone to her bank,
and withdraws just enough money
to get her by till the next check arrives.
She's lived this way since her discharge
from the state hospital. Her yard
is covered with cacti: ocotillo, cholla,
horse crippler, prickly pear, and barrel.
She tends them as one would her roses,
dampening the dust at their base
with just the number of water drops
needed by their precarious suspension
between survival and rot,
till they can make it on their own.
She's never lost a single cactus.
What few times she takes a thorn,
she clips the part outside her skin

and leaves the rest alone, knowing
it will fester for a while and callous over.
Says a little pain makes her feel
so much more alive,
like the drabness of existence here
scintillate with the quirks of character.

VI. The Geologist

As he aged into his fifties,
the frequency of his trips
to Big Bend increased so much
his wife of thirty years
left him for a less impassioned
colleague. Hence, he banked
his modest share of their assets,
secured a part-time job
with the U. S. Geological Survey,
and moved to Study Butte.
For ten years, he's spent
at least four days per week
in the park, studying
the twisted, tortured rock,
strata uplifted and fractured
by rising magma
millions of years cold,
and blocks of large
bodies of rocks dropped
by stresses of faulting
active as recently
as the 1995
magnitude 5.6 earthquake
near nearby Marathon,
rivaling the forces
of his marriage.

VII. The Lawyer

Before moving here,
she changed her name,

paid cash for an acre of desert
and cash for the one-room adobe
she had built on it.
Why she moved here's sheer
speculation, and when asked
she whispers her pat reply:
To let the deceptive
sundown of doing
vanish into the starlit, blue-
black wonder of being.
Some say she had a lucrative
law practice but gave it up,
along with her home, furnishings,
and all her other possessions
when a psychotic client
murdered her husband
and grown, only child.
She wears nothing
but used clothing
sold by nearby charities, drives
an old Jeep the color of the desert,
plays guitar and writes poetry,
and caps off her afternoons
scooted beneath, sparkling
with the sweat of cold beer,
the bar of but mesquite.

VIII. The River Guide

He became a guide
in his late teens, more
from brute necessity
than choice. Over time,
his creased, leathery skin
has assumed the brownish hue
of the river he's guided
thousands of tourists down,
down through the towering,
rock walls of the canyons.
He takes great comfort

in never losing a tourist
to the swirling, anonymous
depths of the river.
When it runs too low for rafting,
he paints and sells pastels
of Chihuahuan Desert scenes
conspicuously absent
the river he knows so well
he could raft it blindfolded.
What little sleep he gets
on the half bed in his shack
is troubled by his dream
of seeing little children
running toward a cliff
above the river:
of his twin, ten-year old brother
slipping from his grip
the way he did that day
he drowned; slipping from his grip
to the raging river
the color of dried blood,
so savage it never spared
his brother's body.

IX. The Artist

Deaf and mute since birth
she came here for the violent
loquacity of light and landscape.
Declared a prodigy at five,

she breezed through school despite
her double handicap, and earned
her M.F.A. summa cum laude.
Soon as she could eke out a stark

living from her art, she came here,
set up a modest gallery,
and stayed. Starting out with oils
and inks executed with mastery,

she quickly turned to working
only in pastels hued with crushed
sundowns, rendering Mother Desert
solely with the gestalt of her clods.

X. Terlingua Graveyard

Though listed in the national register of historic places,
it's owned by the desert flaunting dominion
with creosote, mesquite, live ant beds and prickly pear.
The only care it receives is the footfall of visitors
which over time has made, and kept barren, narrow trails
between the plots. The older graves, of quicksilver miners
long devoid of names, are marked with crumbling stone
or collapsed, wooden crosses. Those of the recent dead
are testaments to the simple things they cherished:
a baseball cap; a little flag; a childhood doll; a paperweight
with swirling snow; desert-caked beer and liquor bottles;
remnants of books loosing flaking pages to the wind;
pinwheels and whirligigs fashioned from the tin of old cans.
The locals destined for their plots here love it,
opting for burial in a pine box, naked save their boots,
happy that their passing's just another party
for their loved ones, another chance to revel in their brief,
sweet lives and return to Mother Desert what was borrowed.

ACKNOWLEDGMENTS

The selected poems in this collection (Sections I, II, and III), some of which were previously published in slightly different versions, are arranged thematically, and were selected from the following volumes:

The Lighthouse Keeper (Timberline Press, 2001): "Crabber," "Brown Pelican," "Ghost Crab," "Old Gull," "In the Nacreous Hours," "The Ferry" and "The Lighthouse Keeper"

Amazing Grace (*Texas Review* Press, 2001): "Palo Duro Canyon," "Herefords in Winter," "The Red Raging Waters," "Rattlesnake Roundup," "Of Dust Thou Art," "Amazing Grace," "Madonna and Child," "The Light of Mexico," "*El Camino del Rio,*" "Warrior Woman," "For Purity," "Tumescence," "Crows Roosting," "Of Eyes Wondrously Wild" and "Primary Colors"

The Woodlanders (Pecan Grove Press, 2002): "Neches River," "Slug," "In the Voodoo Lounge," "Twin Spinsters in Blue," "Tumescence" (also in *Amazing Grace*) and "The Laws of His Kind"

Where Skulls Speak Wind (*Texas Review* Press, 2004): "Wind," "Vultures," "Alzheimer's," "Texas Two-Step," "Kaleidoscope," "Out of the Blue," "A Place in the Sun," "Of Fathers and Sons," "The Night We Were Gods," "Bluing," "Aunt Mae and Uncle Worley's Rocker," "To Blue" and "Road Kill"

Stark Beauty (Timberline Press, 2005): "Rain," "The Skull Seller," "Texas Mountain Laurel," "Over Barbecue," "Bones," "Gabriel," "Harvest Moon," "Cotton," "Spirit Sign" and "Driving Through West Texas"

With the Light of Apricots (published online by Lily Press, 2007): "Artificial Fruit" and "Apricots"

The Fraternity of Oblivion (Timberline Press, 2008): "Of Ceremony," "Even the Moon," "A Big Black Raven," "Colors," "That Glorious Crash," "The Soft Lamps," "She Works Nights" and "From the Dark Swells"

Many of the new poems (Section IV) were previously published in the following journals:

Borderlands: Texas Poetry Review: "Coma"
Curbside Review: "Flaking the Slate Gravestones" (published with
    the title "Not the Nearby Common")
Desert Candle: "Terlingua Graveyard" (strophe X of "Terlingua")
Iron Horse Literary Review: "Crow with Red Sky"
Langdon Review of the Arts in Texas: "Bach"
Lily Literary Review (online): "The Golfer"
Poetry Depth Quarterly: "Woman with a Crow"
RE:AL, The Journal of Liberal Arts: "The Dragonfly"
Red Rock Review: "Minotaur"
Rosebud Magazine: "Hawk"
Small Pond Magazine of Literature: "French Quarter"
Texas Review: "In Maine"

"Alzheimer's." JAMA: The Journal of the American Medical Association
    284: No. 3 (2000): 280. Copyright 2000, American
    Medical Association.

"French Quarter." The Small Pond Magazine of Literature Vol. XXXV,
    No. 2 (103), Beinecke Rare Book & Manuscript Library,
    Yale University. Copyright 1998, Napoleon St. Cyr,
    Editor/Publisher.

ABOUT THE AUTHOR

Larry D. Thomas, who retired in 1998 from a thirty-one year career in social service and adult criminal justice, has published seven collections of poems. Among the numerous prizes and awards he has received for his poetry are the 2004 Violet Crown Award (Writers' League of Texas), 2003 Western Heritage Award (Western Heritage Museum, Oklahoma), two *Texas Review* Poetry Prizes (2004 and 2001), a 2007 Poet's Prize nomination (Nicholas Roerich Museum), two Pushcart Prize nominations, and a $2,000.00 grant from The Ron Stone Foundation (October 2007). In June 2002, he was selected by Barnes and Noble Booksellers as the Houston Area Author of the Month. In spring of 2007, he was named Poet Laureate of Texas for 2008.

LARRY D. THOMAS
NEW AND SELECTED POEMS

ISBN 978-0-87565-360-0

Case. $15.95

TCU TEXAS POETS LAUREATE SERIES

ISBN 978-0-87565-360-0

9 780875 653600   51595